Floodgate Poetry Series Vol. 2

Kallie Falandays

Aaron Jorgensen-Briggs

Judy Jordan

series edited by Andrew McFadyen-Ketchum

Table of Contents

Judy Jordan
Hunger

PREFACE

Andrew McFadyen-Ketchum, Series Editor

The *Floodgate Poetry Series* is published each Fall by Upper Rubber Boot Books.

We are excited to release Volume 2 of the *Floodgate Poetry Series: Three Chapbooks by Three Poets in a Single Volume.* In the tradition of 18th and 19th century British and American literary annuals and gift books as well as series like the Penguin Modern Poets Series of the late 20th century, *Floodgate* uniquely showcases the work of three distinct poets via the chapbook, an oft-overlooked form that captures the essence of a poet's vision and voice.

In bringing together debut collections by Kallie Falandays and Aaron Jorgensen-Briggs with the next collection penned by Judy Jordan, *Floodgate* celebrates the broad range of poetry being written today.

We hope you enjoy this collection of poetry and poets as much as we do.

Tiny Openings Everywhere

KALLIE FALANDAYS

Tiny Openings Everywhere

I Imagine Opening Like a Drawer Full of Old Stockings

It's scary: when I met myself
I was a worry doll,
a tiny tremor, a teacup shaking

until it rains & every thunder
sounds like a winter train:

the water brings up everything
that doesn't have roots

and leaves it all on the floor. See?
After we discover our littleness

we become many different kinds
of hurt.

Tiny Openings Everywhere

If you cut into your belly with a jagged picture frame, I bet you'd find either one rotting plum and a box of yellowed postcards, or you'd find your mother's old stockings. There's nothing there, they'd shout, so that in the afternoon, you'd wake up from your nap and look like a monstered forest: I'm saying a controlled burn. I'm saying one disfigured bird's nest. I'm saying that they're building houses on your dirty land. I'm saying no one cares if they chop you down: it's easier 'cause you're empty. I'm saying take everything to the left of your body and put it in your stomach: giraffe pillow, iPhone case, spray bottle and all. Make yourself whole with things you've touched, but for fuck's sake, don't forget to wash your hands so that when you pray to the stuffing inside of you, you can shine.

[Sometimes the water is staring]

Sometimes the water is staring at you like help me help me. And then your brother calls you from Japan and asks if you know how to spell tsunami; how to say tsunami in Italian. Then everyone on the airplane you are always on looks at you and seems to cry and then all of them say at once *we have been waiting so long to see you* and then when you sleep you begin to dream. Your boyfriend has half of an ear missing. Your cat keeps turning into a dog, turning into a person, turning into a chicken, a coward. You are flying; your cat is a bird and she is flying; your boyfriend still has half of an ear but he can still hear. Then your boyfriend is a blanketed shipwreck; the ocean tried to take him for a moment. Sometimes, the morning looks like a tiny body.

Sometimes We Build Small Ships

and we put them in our pocket

and we hope they sail us somewhere.
Sometimes we build ourselves

large oceans and we pray that they will take us
somewhere warmhearted. Sometimes we carry

on our backs big metal swings and sometimes we rust when it rains.
Most times we eat at regular-sized tables and other days we don't

want to be anything at all and so we make ourselves small.
Sometimes we make solar systems

out of our bruises. We sit on the bed and stare
at our friends and say do you see Taurus? Do you

see milky? Do you see meteor? If we cry sparklers,
our hands feel like they're burning. Sometimes they're burning

and no one has water. Sometimes our friends burn
from the inside out and pieces of them come off on the light switch

and sometimes they sit on our couch

and we can't tell which one is darker.
Sometimes we build tiny loves in our hearts and hope

they become large. Sometimes we pluck them out
through our eyes and name them. Sometimes we forget them

and when we hide they come out and rub our heads and pity us
the way we want to be pitied. And sometimes they build us

and make us large. And hold us up towards the sky
and let it bless us.

And sometimes we make our own morning
and are our own light.

[I believe your eyes]

I believe your eyes
are table colored because when they position

themselves between me and the wall I feel
ground. I lie backwards

to face the sun and can feel the dirt
coming up to meet me. If I lie

and say I do not love the way
your hands hold the wall up,

or say I cannot believe the way the wall bends
to your hands or say you are not the house

because you are the house.
You are also wave.

You are wind drift and cold-
paned window-vines.

You are ocean gray and bully blue:
to say you are not

only wide enough to encompass many maps
but you are the veins

on the maps once they are folded:
not only the memory of the storm

but also the wet dirt on my hands
after I try to wipe you off.

The Last Page in the Book of Sorrows

After I cut apart the monster I discovered myself
crawling. When the darkest building
has no windows. When the crosses burn neon bright
in the early light of evening. When all the poems
were making themselves vomit because they were tired
of hearing it. We are all tired of hearing it. Even the last page
of the last book from the last story will be covered in it
and we will have to use gloves to get to the bottom part—
soggy and tearing. It will not tell us what we need to hear.
We will tell it what it needs to, here: home is here, do not go
anywhere but here. And then we will dry it all off
and we will go home and pretend
that nothing ever happened because we don't want it
to happen again.

[This afternoon, I can't stand]

This afternoon, I can't stand to hate everyone and my memory loves me even when I don't. Even after all of the shitty stuff we've all done. Even after we murdered all of our angels and hung them on sticks and pretended they were Halloween decorations. Even after we roughed our gods around in our mouths until they twisted like cherry stems. Even if we haven't actually lived in a trailer park, we've felt like one, and our grass is yellowed and sometimes we have to borrow our neighbor's water because we broke our hose trying to shove it in our boyfriend's ass or something like that and it's hard to say sorry when you're sorry for everything and then if we go to bed we will wake up mirrored and see ourselves as bleeding angels and some dark-haired boy will come with glue and he will find three dead birds and pluck their feathers and stick them on our backs and say *see see you are still an angel, you're just all sticky.* And then we will go buy a blanket that some machine crocheted and we will pretend our grandmother made it. Or we won't.

Imagine if Everyone You Ever Loved Never Stopped

Touching you. If you never stopped changing: You're still
in your bedroom: blue lamplight, still teenage-hurt,
no alarm clock. How do you get up in the morning
after being held down by so many hands, at least
sixteen of them, each of them trying to draw something
from your body: this one wants a doll
house for his daughter, this one wants to pull out
breakfast, so many breakfasts, so many pieces of toast.
This one wants to pull you into morning, wants to convince you
to come out from under your blankets. They all want you to come
to their house for Christmas. None of them is scared
you'll say no. They'll try to forget about the other hands
and they'll reach around every one else's ring fingers
just to scrape the inside of your mouth
with their thumb, and then they'll say they've captured you,
and then they'll look at your saliva on their finger and they'll put it in
their mouth: no one will think this is wrong
and every one will try it too.

Untranslatable

The word for sitting in darkness
together, waiting for something to burst.

The word for yearning to be
somewhere you are not.

The feeling you're where
you shouldn't be.

The word for when you come home and everything
has changed but the curtains and rugs.

The word for the uncontrollable habit
of thinking everything is a symbol.

The word for the woman who
sits on her doorstep yelling

obscenities at her husband.
I love you. I don't love you.

There is an opening in the doorway,
I might go that way. I might.

There is a mark left on my skin
from your clothes. I love you. The word

for when everything
means something else.

[Everyone is always searching]

Everyone is always searching for their own olive tree
to die under. And once they find it, in a man
or something like it, they'll look at him and say he wasn't as rosy
as he seemed, and then he will die under her olive
tree, and she will have to search for another. But it hasn't happened
yet, so for now, they still water the same flowers and a young girl
sings about morning, and all of the mothers look at her and say
Yes, yes. Always spring and such
and even if they don't mean it, it grows.

Before Before Before

If you were at a dance party and my name rhymed with overalls, would you court me? And then, after we kissed, would you go to your friends to get high fives? If I only wore orange, would you peel me under the blankets like chewed paper falling from the structure of a papier-mâché elephant? Here, pretend like you're an air conditioner. Pretend to pull your dick out at a party. Pretend to get reprimanded. This is what your face looks like when it's hurt. This is what your hands look like when they're bound. This is what you look like when you've discovered yourself the next morning in a city that smells like wet trash. There are two things I'd like to say to you, but I can't find the correct anatomy. It's like searching for ghosts in November. It's like breaking all the wood in the house because it won't light on fire.

[M says that he has a mast on his lungs]

M says that he has a mast on his lungs.
Not a mast, he says, a mass.

I picture a church splitting open over his lungs—
the choir shifting from leg to leg to stable
themselves. I say stable and he pictures wood burning

on the side of a mountain—
all of the people from the rhyme spinning out
like an ocean.

He says open and I hear broken—
the bedroom that we are lounging in is not
a bedroom, it is a woven maple.

We All Blossom in the Morning

And we shove our skin back to say hello there how are you? Are you looking all right? Then we will turn our backs on our backs and go to someone else's home and we will say to their honeys I'm home and after they welcome us—and they will welcome us—we will say what did you make us for dinner, then? And then when we're tired of eating their beef we will find someone else's and we will say to them honey honey and it sounds more bitter than it is.

Stop Stop Don't Walk that Way

All the poems in my dream start with the weather:
either it's raining everywhere or someone is eating
breakfast. Either it's always raining
or something is dying in the bathtub. Either everything
is brighter than a throbbing diamond or your mother is going
to die. Either everyone is a black box hollowing or you are sitting
on the beach. It is never this simple: there are so many bathtubs,
so many oceans opening, so many black cardboard boxes hanging
from ceilings so that when the windows are open and the wind
blows, they hit each other
and no one shatters.

The Tub Drains Like a Fool

& the whole world is chain-clanging down
the halls, all of them screeching
mercy me   mercy mercy   me please mercy me
and then when they find mercy stuck
between the radiator and the wall
they'll go clang-changing down the alleys again screlching along
percy please   percy percy   please and they won't find him anyhow
he's still hanging on to some piped dreams some pillowed mornings
some left lung dispatched a long time ago
and even then everything hollow
hallows itself against the wall calling only for itself and mercying
that wall like a corroding prom date like unrust yourself
like rubbing two fires together will make somebody smooth
and then they'll leave each other mouthing for morning and pulling
all their teeth out with their pliers
and pluggin 'em back up with papers
so that when they bite the dust, neither one of them hurts.

What What Are We Going to Do

I'd lie about my name
if I didn't have one: say call me tomorrow, call me only,
call me after. Twenty-three apples are lying in a field
and every one dies. Where do the birds go?

Once, in the morning, I thought I saw you bleeding.
It was just a shadow of the night trying to fit inside you.
Once, in the storm, I thought I saw my reflection
made out of boat parts; believed my head could sail you;
believed my bones could anchor you.
But with all the waves! What with all the waves?

And past them, and forward, what with all the aching
ship masts? What are we going to do with all these ghosts
and their biting feet; where are we going to hide them

when our lovers come home from work and what
will we say when our lovers say *tell us everything?*

[I dreamt the window was something you held]

I dreamt the window was something you held
inside your mouth. Once again, I woke up
and it was raining. And the rain
made a boat of my body and if I could,
I'd stay a boat forever because of floating
and outside of every window is a man who has been walking
for a very long time and since it's raining, he's cold.
If he could talk, he'd look at you and ask you
if you want to come home or how to get home
and then every time you'd wake up you'd smell like paint
because the man you brought home would have
painted your face like a porcelain doll
and he would coo you to sleep
and say *I've always wanted a porcelain girlfriend.*
I've always wanted a porcelain cloud.
And then he'd try to redo the whole sky
by building porcelain clouds and throwing them towards the sun.

A Room Mostly Full of Deathbeds

We talk brokenly about windows and death
and other things we pretend don't fog up in the morning.
While Bilac asks for coffee and some contemplate the labyrinth,
my grandmother, who is still alive, waits for her husband
to hold her hand again.
Dalí wonders where his clock is (inside of him all along)
while Mahler dies shouting "Mozart,"
and Anna Pavlova wants her swan
costume ready. Only one asks
if you could turn the light out. And most
of them, like I might, die
asking if you hear the rain.

The Woman Holy of Anatomy

Her iliac crest borders the wing of ilium.
She is hungry and is trying to eat her skin.

The brim of her pelvis is apple shaped.
She cannot say why she has a lesser pelvis,

only that it aches. The hard palate of her mouth
becomes soft from sucking sour candy in the evening.

Her uvula continues to vibrate
even after she stops screaming. What she does

with her hands is akin to bating.
She perches on the porch like a mermaid

thumbing. It's difficult to tell whether she sleeps
with her distal phalanges in the fetal position.

She mouths things to herself in the mirror:
Fimbria, shallow, symphysis. She cannot get filled.

One Dream Opening into Many

My mother hobbles through the door.
It is Sunday, but today hasn't happened yet.

There is a bluebird dying in a cherry tree.
Next to my window, its loose feathers reveal

wrinkled skin. This bird,
which is also not a bird, is still dying

though, at times, when my mother hobbles
past the window to the door,

the sunlight clouds its feathers, its beak,
its tiny hands like tiny people

made of light stepping over the ocean
and it is set free.

Illumination

Memory: a bird crashed through the window.
Truth: I mourned for you without speaking.
A shadow of the bird crashed through the window.
Here I mourned for you. Without speaking.
Yesterday: A bird crashed. Through the window,
I mourned for you. Without speaking
truth. A shadow of the bird crashed through the window.
I mourned for you here. Without speaking.
Without speaking you must believe me,
a bird and its shadow crashed through the window.
It will happen again, you must believe me.
I mourned for you through the window.
It is dusk and I dream of flight.
Then of my own death. I dream of flight.

ABOUT KALLIE FALANDAYS

Kallie Falandays is currently living in Philadelphia. You can read more of her work in *PANK, Salt Hill, Black Warrior Review, Tupelo Quarterly*, and elsewhere.

ACKNOWLEDGEMENTS

Kallie Falandays would like to thank *Wicked Alice, Black Warrior Review, Forklift, Ohio, Deluge, Banango Street, Likewise Folio, Ohio Edit, The Poetry Storehouse,* and *Miriam's Well* where some of these poems appeared.

Score for a Burning Bridge

AARON JORGENSEN-BRIGGS

Score for a Burning Bridge

The Names

I.

Don't I know you from somewhere
I said to the abandoned fountain.

Come home with me
I said to the echo.

Little birds
darted from tree to tree.

There was a scent of seawater,
there was a childhood memory, and weeds

sighed
like slender women. A paper bag was happy and

the purr of locusts—like something seen
from very far away.

II.

This was long after the names had gone.
Not gone, exactly, but

having come to the end of desire
were finally free to be themselves.

So that at night, sometimes
when stars shone on the water

and the water held still,
you might hear voices.

Once, I heard my mother's voice.
She was still a girl, and her laughter

was mouthfuls of fruit.

8th Street

Then I found myself
inside a house. Alone in the dark,

the door half-open. The path I had taken
rolled back like a wave.

Sunlight touched the windowsills,
reminding me

of other rooms. I knew
that iron stove, the smell of apples,

rooms she tried to mend
with pale, Victorian roses, a mouthful of pins.

Rooms where he tried
on windless afternoons, at the piano or the saw.

When the rains came, we slept in the cellar
with the turtles, in their resinous silence.

If it was not that house, it held
as still, while morning settled

on the blue bay in the Chinese fire screen,
where the boatman leaned

into the room, and I was a fleck
on that horizon.

Iowa

Around the lake they built their houses.
They planted grain

behind the houses, where the children sometimes
discovered each other,

hiding their bodies and their cries
through all kinds of weather.

I believe it was sunny
the day my father fell

between the rows, where she had fallen.
A jet may have passed

far behind his head, or a crow
may have brushed a quick shadow

across her face, dividing the day
into before and after. In either case

they lie there still, unspeaking. And though
they will not touch again,

I often dream of flight.

D.

The car had started fine, I remember
white frost on the windshield, blackbirds

on snow. My mother's hands
were white also. Her cigarette

and veil of smoke. My breath
on the window

when she spoke
the word that made the morning

stutter. Frozen
grass outside the school,

the strange language everyone spoke
all day, with their tiny mouths.

The switchblade a boy let me touch
for fifty cents. That clean sound

and the silence after.
Home again, faint laughter

on TV, a whorl of smoke
beneath the lampshade

where she read a book. This is
that story.

Salt (I)

I know this town, I know this dusk, quiet
as a coat on a hook. I am meant to believe
a street should be this clean.

So say these poker-faced houses
insisting with perfect composure
that everyone's at home.

Sometimes I sidle past, my name
like a pill on my tongue. Sometimes I steal
an egg's worth of grief.

Then houses shift in their moorings,
I stand on a pier, unable to reckon
how each is tethered

to its story of passage, how each tows
its allotted sea.

Salt (II)

Second bell. The nets are empty. The map
is drunk. The angel on the prow
grows tired of the zodiac.

I light another cigarette and pace
an acre of lamplight
in a small white room where nothing happens.

Sometimes I stand all night
on the doorstep, unable to enter
the cabin in the keyhole. Tonight

the map is angry, the map is lost
inside the act of folding.
It takes the form of a taxi, a horse.

I write my name beside the island
shaped like a fist.

Christmas Past

We stood on the bridge, in the snow
watching cars appear—
lit matches, then

candles, floating on water.

I thought of winter in Benares: sooty
morning fog, butter-colored votives lifting
the names of the dead.

And then, because you wore your houndstooth coat,
I thought of Dickens' grave.
The night held many cities.

Home again, the opened gifts in the living room
had nothing left to say
and nowhere they were needed. Each held

a portion of the night.

Nathan

Sixteen and you
meant bad, cousin. Took me
with you, part of a summer

watching you filch tokens
from the till at the arcade,
skinny bottles of Mad Dog

in the pockets of all your friends,
that black Camaro,
the nights still and warm.

I didn't understand
why we had to slip
through the narrow window

in whispers and dew
to rage against the empty streets,
ghost-drag through town

with heads full of metal, smoke
in our eyes. Clatter of milk
crates behind the Safeway

where you hollered sweet
nothings, in sodium light.

Sonnet with words from a soft drink bottle

Perhaps it was a lack of vitamins.
Perhaps it was the absence of a button
to press, a legless robot to set the table,
to clear it away when the meal was forgotten,
when the guests had gone home. Dessert
in lemon-colored capsules, pink Chiclets
of me-time, conveniently bite-sized. Or else
a drinkable Swiss Army knife. Something
decisive, all-in-one. Instead, this treadmill
and erector set. This irresponsible
flying car. This broken clutter I've invented,
my laborious docudrama, my theoretical
framework, this crippled coat-tree,
this movie poster where I pay the rent.

Democracy

On the night of the election an egregious insect
was misinformed in my kitchen. In the mouth of morning
there was still a dream about a girl. I had swallowed
a multivitamin and trapped the dream under a jar.
It once held, as the results came in, maraschino cherries.
The girl and the insect got in a fight. I voted for the girl
but the insect was a tiny, ravenous machine.

Brooklyn

Close enough to the piazza one detected fragrances, minute vibrations of thirsty females. We all got slightly high, clutching each others' shapely fists. Lots of us were wearing striped shirts. I needed sunscreen, remarkable foodstuffs, a suit made of medicine. Faithfully new trucks arrived, departed bearing sufficient leather.

I carried a briefcase all that summer. The least I could do, lacking silkier motifs. I thought it might rain, we all did. We all forgot several items on the way to the store. Stylish glasses failed to compensate for maternal absences. We felt sticky as candy, with grit in our teeth. Attempts at frankness would not ignite a more rigorous discourse, dinosauric tactics along the wall-tops, for the city suffices, inflicts its daily regimen of small, cosmetic alterations to the basic fact.

That all winter we've been thoroughly pooped. That a woman looks familiar but is unknown, anonymously ogled in parking lots surrounded by empty carts, apparently sleeping, dreaming of gasoline and thoughtful gifts. Meanwhile, drum machines inject balletic sabotage throughout this two-party system. Confounding fathers ply their wares tiptoe, high-fiving in public restrooms, fixing colorful wheels to their sternest shoes. Likewise I have often driven, dreaming, a diesel contraption, chiseled and sullen, nearly erotic. Men speak on TV of ballistic implications, sufficient mathematics to injure self-regard, recent wardrobe choices.

It could have been worse. The application of scented ointments, delicate, sanguinary, the stuff of migraines. Tolerant adornments, a diversity of methods. Four defenseless varieties, or hues of paper, or papery satisfactions, a new sort of sexual physics, a language consisting of pleasurable touches below the knee, such things as render us unshod. Poorly attired for sleep, we walked the streets well past midnight, aroused by lunar pantomime.

I mean the code was written on a series of napkins, progressive drunkenness prerequisite to any conception of the good life. Time itself grew yellow, bright as lemons, thoroughly washed and salted. A fruit one lived inside, as well as one could. Smoky gazes traveled the horizon, a matter of perspective, locomotion for its own sake. Whenever we touch we are one soft machine. I have not claimed otherwise. Repeat the song but it will end the same, with stolen fanfare. A childhood recollection is not the same as the throat's hoarse knowledge. What things taste like, which shadows sustain.

The shadows or the nets brought down small creatures with iridescent wings, enough to comprise evidence of fraud, the opposite of pleasure. Ironic conclusion to a dance I even bought shoes for. Now I'm stuck with my pen in my hand, don't feel like pedaling faster. A muscular confusion. And though I might describe it lovingly, my Facebook friends have other galleries from which to gather doomed and guilty looks.

But not for long. In seconds, planetary motion casts a shifting light upon our snack times. I have purchased the accoutrements suggested by our finest chefs, though some remain untelevised. Regardless, I intend to finish my series of missionary poses, all the while pretending to have done this before, casually remarking on some blonde's apparent lack of closure. Despite my best intentions, many stones were left in the garden. What was needed: a tiny horse, a tiny plow.

Voyeurism

It's happened again. I'm standing
at the kitchen window, lost
inside a map of Sunday, something cold
and distant in my hand.

The young couple
that lives across the street—I have seen
the TV rinse her body blue,
her lover in his ragged beard.

The parrot on the windowsill
stabbing at fruit.
The thing I'm looking for
is never in the parrot's beak,

just the hard little finger
of its dry, articulate tongue.

Once

I was a Portuguese sailor.
Out of luck on the jetty, the tip
of my last cigarette tempted the sun
into the water.

That was you among the wives,
returning under the first net of stars,
what you carried still desperate
to be alive.

When the moon strode clear
to shore, I knew I could follow you.

In your husband's house, the cutlery
was sleeping. The fish
lay on the table, a heap of coins, in every eye
the clear, cold premise of a star.

Year of the Rooster

There was a palm tree
but coconuts had been tied on. A sputtering
of plastic fronds, an implausible,
lame tutu. The burnish of aluminum teapots,
that was something. The paper lanterns
dozing, held their light. I wanted to confide

in the fastidious waiter, his hair
groomed into something reliable.
He looked like he would have
a decent singing voice.
I wanted to make desperate love
to every girl in every minidress

in month after month of calendar photos,
no matter how improbable the gondola,
the parasol. Girls with such enterprising hats
always in danger of blowing away
like the pages of a calendar,
with the sound of a harp.

It was February, I went on missing you.
Children threw fire at the wind.

Reply from Oslo

Cigarettes in silver boxes,
pale flashes of mood
at a corner table.

The tall girl roosts
beside me in the dark,
her hands form a cradle

she stares into, a portrait
of her wedding day in Kragero,
where waves eat the coast.

A month from now
you will send a letter.
You too will have married

a sober engineer
on a windy cliff. And I
will have finished my poem

with a puzzling digression
on cartography, by which
I mean to suggest

I have found a passage
North, I have left
the last of our cities.

Still life with carrot, stick

When you had gone, the platform stunk
of violins and other men's luck.

Then there were parties, and east-
bound trains, late drunks outside the clubs,

cigarettes in blond light. As if anyone needed
another homeless cocktail dress,

another melancholy frotteur. One more story
of trains and speeds, the distance

to another man's wife. Got back
to my dirty pictures. All next day

there was heat, there were breezes
plucking skirts. I rode the F

to Coney Island. Jeweled bellies on the beach,
the sea locked tight

the way a woman hides her mouth
and calls it laughter. The way a man vanishes

inside the heat of a kiss, night after night
the way he searches

there, and calls it marriage.

Score for a Burning Bridge

Between you and somewhere, stopped
in Michigan, where all the waitresses
were plotting lost loves, their eyes

gone walking
through picture windows, washed-out
parking lots like Polaroids

of parking lots. I thought of you, a girl
I've known forever, the weight of summer
in your eyes, pinned by camera

to solar flare

◊

Drinking my drink, strange women tumble
under broken ice. My long face wavers, moon
in a glass-bottom boat.

When you are here, the shattered light
makes sense, softens into simple language, neon
shrapnel buffed by a sea

◊

All night of swimming
your marvelous train
threads the sealight. I mean your breath

is the wavering torch
on the hillside, what the night chases
when breezes rattle and ignite.

I mean the sealight, breathing you
is green, and the night

a needed fiction, a way of insisting

to have met you, there
in a room as simple as a tear

◊

My memories of the encounter.
The young lawyer was surprisingly hostile.
Had wavy jet black hair.
The subject was the nature of love.
I argued that love could only be for a specific person.
She argued that one could love all mankind.
We talked about Natasha from *WAR & PEACE*.
I did not enjoy the experience

◊

Something with a girl in summer: dreamed
of Connie Francis by a swimming pool in heart
-shaped glasses, regal and aloof. A hotel
pool, with elevator chime and brassy
potted fern, her scarf
blue-bright, like everything

◊

A sky is clotted
smoke: blame it
if your lungs shiver
for cigarettes of foreign
ladies. All the parks are full of chess
and litter.
Keep a weather eye
on the magician's left hand. Kiss me
here, while night is still
possible

◊

Some birds have left
their hollow flutes
in the pornographer's tree

as if to say *you have nothing to fear*
now we are flightless

◊

This girl comes up to me
the other night, breathing gin,
offering a filthy palm
so empty it looks almost
weightless.

Fish my pockets, searching
her muddy eye

◊

I don't remember
when a man first touched me,
he wore a white coat.
The knife in his hand

a key, a hole he carried
and gave to my body
a piece of the night, an opening
where time rushed in, dragging my name

◊

My father taking off
his belt. His paintbrush mustache
reminds me of someone. His powder
blue suit reminds me.

I didn't even go
to the prom, but there I am
by the punchbowl, a face in a cup,
his frilly white shirt

◊

And you were there. Your sullen shadow
walked the waves, like it was no big deal
to leave you standing

with the wind dividing your hair
in the dusk, with your back to the sea,
apprenticed to it

◊

On Valentine's Day
I take Plato to the Ziegfeld
to see *Iron Man 2.* He is delighted
by the apparatus, how it resembles
his idea. He imagines himself, the tiny
theater inside his eye.

And then I take the butterfly poet
to see Lauren Bacall, and he weeps
at the sight of her bottom lip.

After, we go to Chinatown and drink
sweet coffee under paper
lanterns

◊

As per the unleashing
of wild creatures—

Exit interview

Was it a rain-coaxed sleep
or a feathery mask?

In a thief's attire
I watched you shift and utter.

Your tongue, was it the cause of blindness
or a dance intended as a cure?

This would explain the hoof-beaten tempos
my blood concocted

for your rumorous mouth.
But whose dream was this

and what were its requirements?
Bedragglement, a gibbous charm, a taste

that wine had sharpened
till it tore at your skirt.

At dawn, what shimmied
down the bed-sheets and fled? A kiss

like the broken back of something
small, in the mouth of a cat.

ABOUT AARON JORGENSEN-BRIGGS

Aaron Jorgensen-Briggs lives in Des Moines, Iowa where he is a member of the Des Moines Catholic Worker community. He maintains a blog (poorly) at http://flotson.net.

ACKNOWLEDGEMENTS

Aaron Jorgensen-Briggs would like to thank *dirt* and *Gumball Poetry*, where poems in *Score for a Burning Bridge* first appeared.

Hunger

JUDY JORDAN

Hunger

These First Mornings Living in the Greenhouse

I wake with a fine snow of my own breath
laced across my face, a stranger's name scratched
on the ice-slaked plastic, and swinging above
my head, the wrist-thick rope from which I pull
myself from bed. Sun crawling over the pines
prisms through the interior frost and turns it to water
and fog so that the greenhouse becomes a phantom of itself.
Mist rises, ice melts, plants unfurl from their cold,
wet sleep to stretch and finger steam
as the sun staggers higher and shafts of light
swell and tumble and skirr
through the drizzle. Then the plants blink,
                                        fully awake,
their veined blood beating faster,
and the greenhouse opens like a bleached eye.

Into Light, Into Another Day

Even before half the greenhouse buckled
from the weight of back-to-back wet winter snows,
the design was nebulous: hollow steel curved

into arcs then screwed into four-by-fours and pine studs.
A high school gym's surplus shower curtain
was strung aft to aft and rope-rigged

just where the steel had bent and broke
to salvage the half of the greenhouse which still
curved like a translucent egg against wind and cold.

Floundering ship that never keeps out water or leaves its moorings.

But still it is a simple enough idea, the half
of the greenhouse with the huge gas heater crumpled,
steel snapped, plastic ripped, peeled back, flapping in wind,

so where to go but to the other half: the cot
I sleep on, rising every two hours to chunk wood
into the brick-lined fifty-five gallon drum, the annuals

and perennials leaf-dark from cold, shifting a little
when the warm air sifts and fingers
through the tangle of bedding flats.

Each gust of wind rips the greenhouse plastic
from the frame, then slams it back down
so that bedding shelves and hanging baskets shudder

and I grow to believe this tattered plastic
is the loose skin that separates the worlds and I feel
expectant, self-conscious, aware of an unknown gaze,

waiting for something, perhaps death, to reach through
the salt shore of my skin and jerk that unknown part
of me through my mouth's roof to blasted air,

to a place I imagine smells scrubbed and like wild roses
and fog curling from a flooded field at two AM one morning
in May, cows restless in the distance, flooded creek hurling past.

But now I know only the frog's moans under
the bed, lightning-felled tree sending out fresh
stems all along its trunk, green furl of new

plants, tender and moist, and that smell, unnamable
and new, something clean, reborn, stretched from
somewhere, some strange and waiting place, to here.

◊

Plate, spoon, knife, cast-iron pan.
Rope I pull myself up with. Futon,

pillow, seams bleeding feathers,
desk lamp hanging by its cord

from the metal hoops beside the one
pair of dress pants, the sun-splotched coat,

water hose coiled on the ice-slivered gravel:
how I name myself now. And this:

> flats of plants, flats of bone-flecked wet, black loam,
> slim seeds slipped into soil so rich it breathes.

◊

Through plastic, the winter sun looks like polished stone
and all of outside is washed in a strange yellow light,
roof of clouds unbroken and full of rain.
I work all morning, elbow deep in sphagnum and peat moss,

StoneheadBigBeefSnowCrown
PrimeroNapoletanoMarjoramSweet
TequilaSunriseValenciaMortgageLifter

Skies crosshatched in cold drizzle, sun gauze-wrapped
as the ground rises, returning from the snow stone by stone,
wind filled with the wing beats of crows,
earth stirring, shifting a little beneath my feet.

TurkishOrangeRosaBiancaDiamond
DixieGoldenQuadratod'AstiRossi
TennesseeCheeseBloodyButcherBoxcarWillie

If clouds are the clothes of gods hung out to air,
then today it's the lesser gods whose rags bunch
and tangle along the lines of heaven's alleys,
tied window to soot-grimed window.

SweetMillionCaroRichSiamQueen
BigBoyLemonBoyBetterBoy
JetsetterMuchoNachoFinoVerde

On days like this my body unhinges: this focus on particulars,
this disappearance into pain, teaching me what death is,
tumbling me out of myself as I lay another seed flat along

the wood shelves gray with age, then pull myself up,
though sometimes the baseball bat beating of pain is so great,
I think that surely something else tugs me into light, into another day.

BigBerthaEarlyGirlSweetBabyGirl
BrandywineCaspianPinkCelebrity
LavandulaAngustifoliaNepetaCataria

Stretched out now, seeds sipping soil and water,
transplants' bruised roots tender and dependent
as infants incubating under this artificial sky

and as I throw more wood on the fire, raise and lower

the pump's handle, turn the hose to the finest mist, outside
rain begins to fall, earnest and steady, to the snow-

saturated earth, tunneling through mud and roots
and burrows of shivering mice and falling on raptors scouring
the fields for those mice, on worm and cardinal and starling,

on ratsbane and rats alike, rain to rise again, surely as the dead
on their last walk, their trek across the trail of stars
we call the Milky Way, soon to rise again, rise to air,

stumbling along as all things must, on this light-dazzled,
star-spangled bridge of terror we say yes to,
this thing we call life, lucky, lucky, labyrinth of life.

That First Spring

All the rain has spawned frogs.
Puddles birth them and the night
throws cicadas out of its cave
by the fistfuls. Pugnacious night.
Full of terror. Faint traces of mold inch
up the eggplants, their stalks lightning-lit.
Each tree, each weed, each quack grass
and henbit starkly visible, cut silhouettes against
the sky, before the crash of thunder and darkness.
All day the hawk hunted the fields
and near woods, calling like a frightened child.
Just once, even just for this night, I wish
all this scrabbled need would stop. Grasshoppers,
thumb-large, bony, cognizant-faced, mouths chewing
side to side, thump as regular as heartbeats,
moving less than a fingernail's width, all day,
all night, dying, trapped between the shade cloth
and the plastic murky with mildew. The few
lucky ones slip just far enough over the roof's curve,
lose footing, and slide down the greenhouse
into the mint bed with a sound like blood
swooshing through a faulty heart valve.
It's true. A dream is the only reason I keep going.
I'm still searching the creek bank for the stone
I need to swallow to kill the giant creature
in my chest who keeps the words I need
to describe this life hidden under its wings.
Stricken life. Stricken dream. Get up and limp
into a stranger, holding out your hands,
opening and closing your mouth, uttering
those small mewlings, those animal sounds.

After the Farmer's Market

In this hoofed hour before dawn,
              in the flustered scuttle of small animals,

in underbrush and leaf flutter intent in their clawed search.

Shot moon and scumbled cloud, screech owl and bobcat scream.

Moth, bat, and souls of the newly dead flitting leaf to leaf.

In the smell of honeysuckle and angel heart,

in the tick of each star clicking off
and darkness drifting
toward its concession to day's factory of heat and glare,

wake, wake, rise and go
through these empty streets to meet that sunrise
of smelted coins hot with the grief of many hands.

Wake, wake, wake,
              get up, get up, and go now.

In this hour of terror,
              birds crying out,
crying to the blood, to the bitter reek,
to the spilled guts of the night's hunted,

scattered chirps and screeches sifting in wind,
rustling through tree limbs, easing down like a preened feather
to settle in the nests of woven grasses and weeds.

In this hour of the dead,
              get up, get up, and go.

Prowl the steaming, empty streets. Follow the bristle-brushed
truck along the dreary wave of asphalt as the grumbling,
diesel-belching beast hoses yesterday into the gutters.

Get up and go past the rail yard and feed stores,
past the vestibules and crumbling doorways of hunger and no sleep,
past the drunks swaying on the curb's edge,
cabbies getting high in their cars as they wait out the hours,
                                    the horrible and lonely hours.

Now, in the crooked teeth of dawn,
in the growl and lolling tongue,
                            everything else must wait.
The runaways who scour parking lots,
                        heel-to-toe,
for any dropped thing,

ghosts of the black-owned businesses, barbershops
and doctor's offices bulldozed to build this pedestrian mall,

ghosts who hover here with the blue fog,
ghosts squeezed fish-eyed under the ridged mountains,
ghosts slipping along this street with its lobbed and slab-sided
board and batten and drywall houses, must wait.
                                        Ghosts
who climb up the slink and squeak
of the narrow steps to the one-room,
fourth floor walk-up where Ming-Loy shares a cot
with her five-year-old daughter who must wait,
                wait for the tea kettle to scream out,

wait for Ming-Loy to pour this long lick of sinewy water over her
crouched in a tin bucket, wait for her to say, *Broken plumbing.*
Cheap rent,
                wait for the leftovers I will take her,

vegetables, cut flowers, it all, it all, it all must wait now
for I must get up, get up, rise and go.

                Home at three AM
from the pizza delivery job, up at five with the shrieking birds.
Get up and go.

            Oh do not think
of how little will be made, six hours in the heat-scorched lot,
            bone-honed blade of exhaustion

edging up the ladder of my back
with my small offerings of coneflowers,
                              tomatoes and yellow squash
curled in on themselves like question marks,
for the sweating hoards of dimes and nickels,
                              damp wrinkle of dollar bills,
just get up, get up, pack the truck and go.

◊

The letter, picked up off the street said,
so I've found you. What you're doing is time. Jail time
is the longest time. When I see you again it won't be in there
but out here. Here's a twenty for you. Say goodbye
to Toto. We're not in Kansas anymore.

◊

The gout-legged man resting on the bench said,
You have to keep one leg out of your pants
when you take a crap. So you don't get trapped.
That's what you have to do in jail.

◊

The man shouted into his cell phone, *That's what I get*
for trusting damned, no-good, lazy, white trash.

◊

And Luna, who sold incense and hand-made soap, is dead.

And Regina, the muffin-queen, who waited a year
so Blue Cross would cover her back's busted disc,

ignoring blood in her stools, cancer's filed teeth
gnawing along her colon, is dead.

◊

I have seen the women piling from their pimps' Caddies,
seen them spread through the streets
like a rare virus seeping organ to organ,
have seen the sheriff's notice nailed on the door, RENT PAST DUE,

family photos, marksman medals, all the trivia of years
and lives the landlord hauls to the dumpster, ground up
by the trash truck as if in Polyphemus' gaping jaws,
have seen the heavy-booted men splattered with concrete,

hunched at the bar, dull-eyed through the sitcom's canned laughter,
their entire lives laid out before them like a rough-stitched corpse
trundled into its cold slot after the coroner's knife,
and I, no Lazarus, sores licked by dogs, not wrenched

from Abraham's arms, not risen from the dead to warn
the rich man's brothers, only a piping voice that begs the stars
to cast their cold, lidless gaze onto me as I plead that I not die
in such a wrong time, such a wrong place.

◊

Now the sun directly overhead so I must
reload the unsold coreopsis, drooping columbine,
                    vegetables, sun-bruised and soft,
even as they come,
                    those who know the closing hours,
who know the cull of bruised peaches and over-grown squash.

They spill from their rust-shot four-doors,
cars held together with tar, duct tape,
                              clothes hangers and string.

Washed in this warped and ruined light,

a dime store daubing, a bad draft,
I wait here and want to know what happened
to that life I signed up for,
the one with chubby cheeks and blonde hair,
            the freckle-spattered nose and easy smile.

I wait and watch as they wave away yellow jackets
from the mesh-metal trash cans, watch
string-haired teenagers turn their backs on mothers
who pull out worm-gnawed eggplant and yellowing cucumbers.

                Oh how fragile, how frail
this thing we call a body: How desperate and tender
it all seems: Those scant few years ago
when I stood outside any fast food joint,
            too skinny, gulping the grease stink,

and just last year, lugging boulders, splitting wood, then, the burst
    disc,
        pain tunneling down my hamstring,

and now these sullen teenagers, pacing
this parking lot, pretending not to know
their own mothers whose arms are swallowed
by trash cans, who scratch their nails against the melon's mushy rind
and I hold out the blood-red tomatoes, the milky corn:

                Come, I whisper,
come, I cry out like some ancient song, a song of hunger,
                    song of sorrow,
and they creep from the trash cans, the wrecked cars, the blind alleys,
creep from all the hiding places of the poor,
as hunger, musk-mouthed hunger, lumbers from its dark doorway.

Learning to Walk

Surely the body's unlearning
   is hardest: the busted disc, that clutch of fire
working to a floundering limp, first the right leg
   dragging ground, then the left.
But what was that when I became paralyzed, pain

so bad it snapped the thread that tethered the blue sigh
   of my soul, and I floated into air
to stare down at the woman lying in bed,
   unable to comprehend
how she could possibly be me, shivering in a reasty film

of sweat and spasms, passing out, unable to stand or walk.
   While I was unconscious, my soul returned,
only to leave again when I woke screaming. Now,
   after surgery, in the pool, my body's weight buoyed
by water while the muddied twinges of my mind

ooze the messages toward my legs to *kick*.
   Sideways, now *front.*
Then *stand* and—it was a long time before I could
   do this—*on tiptoe.* And on the treadmill,
my arms taking weight, the sludged word *walk,*

what that used to mean.
   That woman lying in bed, her screams,
that bit of me that remained when I disappeared
   I can barely remember. In that time
of unemployment and paralysis and pain so bad my brain

has hidden the memory deep in the coils of itself,
   it was my father
who balanced just on the frame's edge.
   His mind slipped to a place
no one else could go though no one knew why—

Was it the anesthesiologist's clumsy hand, bad mixture

of drugs, series of small strokes,
the liver's animal-fury for more liquor? We'll never know
  though my small mouth cries
out to the other small mouths for any answer.

When I was a child, there was a place inside myself I'd go,
  a switch severing my mind
from my heart, so even with his drunken curses
  what might have been understanding
for him shut down to nothing.

My father's a decade dead as I trudge this artificial path,
  learning to walk again, at each bumbled
step begging forgiveness from whatever waits ahead.
  Not that it matters.
My body knows what I did.

Night Walk, After Surgery, October

Slowly I begin again to believe in my body
as I walk the dirt lane that two months ago
spasmed me to my knees to clutch the ditchweed.
Ditches choked with aster, fields afloat in purple mist.
Wind picks up, clouds crumble off and already
trees creak as they tighten against tonight's cold.

My first words when the med student shouted me
out of ether's haze were "What time is it?"
which is to say, "What span of my star-allotted time is forever gone?"
And my next, "What day?" not believing it possible,
my life only shortened a few hours.

What is this fear, this preemptive sorrow
so unlike what I've been witness to all summer?
Mayflies rise into air in the day's last light,
                              all that wail and struggle,
only to mate then die by midnight.
Moths born without mouths, a few hours of brilliant flight
through the insect-buzzing world,
bumble bees drowsing to a late summer death,

and these staggering yellow jackets, stumbling across
creek-rock and the road's ruts and wheel cuts,
spinning in dust,
                    too cold-stunned to sting,
while the queen sleeps, thousands of lives coiled within her,
bodies of this season's thousands, their black coats
and gold scarves strewn and scattered across the soil.

Nature in her extravagance,
                              nature in all her careful thrift.

Hunger Moon

Three times a day I hobble to the garden,
stare at the leafing world going on around me,
and though all my exquisite care won't
make the plants grow any faster,
I pluck out the pale, small weeds spreading
through the rows. Grass, sneezeweed, bindweed—
tunneling their pale roots through the rot-rich dirt.

◊

The letter said Above and beyond—
   hospital bills, surgeon's fees—the usual
and customary charges
the insurance company would not pay,

which I, after months of paralysis and semi-paralysis,
underemployment and unemployment, could not pay

and they made no difference, all the long-distance
   phone calls to the unskilled number
punchers in their particle-board cubicles
   with their telephones and narrow chairs,
with their futures laid open to the surgeons
   of bad backs and carpel tunnel.

◊

The letter said, *The hospital has seized
         your bank account.*
         The next letter: a court date
to plead your case.

And from the bank:
         funds seized   account frozen.
         The next letters, all the bounced checks.
   Insufficient funds.

No money
      to cover checks already written.
             Insurance payment.
    Truck payment.
        Credit card.
     Credit card.
        Credit card.

A nation of people who take out bank loans
      to buy groceries.

◊

Fifth day without food, I limp to the garden, compost
of horse manure and sawdust, rich as rotten wrist bones,
hilled and greening, corn, razor-edged, knee-high,
scratch of summer squash, leaves palm-big, bulging
with water and sun, cucumber vines,
their fine tendrils climbing the wire trellis.

How long before the green field bursts
in yellow bloom, before those upturned trumpets
of flowers fill with bristle and hum, fill
with the pollen hunting hunger of bees?

◊

Late cold snap, just above freezing.
The unemployment line snaking out
the office door leaves us in gusting wind
and scarce spits of rain. In front of me,

a thin-shouldered boy huddles in his windbreaker,
sharing his last cigarette with his girl. *Shit*,
he says, when the wind tears through clouds and rain begins,
a steady drizzle that pastes his dark curls

to his head. *Shit*, he says, but not like he means it
but as a habit, like cigarettes, like an unemployment line,

like giving up in the gray cold, turning
from his girlfriend and squaring his shoulders,

like the sweater I pull down to hide
the raveled thread where the button has popped off
my slacks, the slow disintegration
on this seventh day without food, already begun.

◊

Dandelion weeds, rotten food dug from garbage dumps, children
so hungry, they chewed off their own fingertips,
  whole families
      living in sewer pipes.
Bowlegged children—
              pellagra, rickets.
The child looked listless.
              The child said she was hungry.
  The child told her teacher
         she couldn't go home and eat.
It was her sister's day to eat.

◊

Yet I keep thinking of the spider,
how she weaves her web from herself,
tufts of thread spooling from her abdomen.
Silk glands. Spinnerets. Boneless, she grows and eats
her outer skeleton to ease the shedding of skin.
These shed lives one sees everywhere
yet never notice—

◊

Less than a decade ago, nights I walked to the end
of Mill Road, climbed the gate posted No Trespassing
then stumbled past the old factory, its broken windows
sprouting Virginia creeper, and joined the others.

Spillway and old dam. Spunk wood
and rusted burn barrels. Stones where cans of soup
or beans bubbled in the small fires. Ground always damp
and sometimes in the morning nothing to eat

but fibers ripped from corn stalks pulled from the Rivanna's
eddies and pools that had washed down
in flood. But, always, someone could rummage
deep in pockets or coat linings for a few
coins and join you at the diner a mile's walk
for a shared cup of coffee, and always, with sugar and cream.

It never leaves you. That life. Why else covet
abandoned barns, drain pipes, and keep always an awareness
of tin cans, how they can be hammered flat, whole cities
of cardboard boxes, scrap wood, and can roofs.

Carolina cotton fields, red clay and sauerkraut,
stone horizons painted the blue of bruises.

And the long walk to the river.

Broken tombstones, turnip greens. Grandfathers
twisted like the necks of hens, mothers fattened like hogs.
Fried chicken and fatback, cow jowl and pig's feet,
hog brains scrambled with eggs, tender meat of squirrels,
a side of hominy and the long walk to the river.

And from the river we come.

Unemployment lines and welfare offices,
grease barrels, slammed dumpster lids.
Blackbird screech in the beaten air.

And from the river we come.

◊

Only four years ago, two-thirty AM

after delivering pizzas for hours,
instead of crawling into the back of my truck to sleep,
I'd walk the quiet neighborhoods in the bug-light
of buzzing street lamps and stare into shadowed living rooms.
Sometimes in the blue glow of the television or a bulb left
burning somewhere deep in the hidden interior, I'd see
their plush couches, chairs, book-lined walls, pianos laced
with doilies, the wall a puzzle of silver frames. Sometimes
I'd sit on their front porches as cats prowled the shrubbery
and slinked yard to yard. At these times I could imagine
myself invisible, could imagine the thwonk of the morning
paper on the steps, people in the houses waking, running water,
making coffee, spit of eggs in grease.

                        Could imagine no one seeing me
when I rose stiff and cold and entered
their front doors to bring news from the other world,
to run my fingers across leather-bound spines,
to fog photos and the fine-polished wood
of the pianos with my boned breath.
Though the one thing I could not imagine, could not remember
or trace to the poorly read map of my life
was how I got there, sitting on strangers' steps,

                            sleeping in my truck,
anymore than I could have imagined living in a greenhouse,
money seized for unpaid hospital bills, anything worth anything,
                 hocked, pawned, sold,

too ashamed to beg a sandwich from a neighbor,
no money for gas to get to that downtown office
with its vouchers for rubbery cheese and white rice,
so that more and more I imagine it true—
on this, my eleventh day without food—

                    my own invisibility,
my bones so porous, so brittle, I would break if touched,
my body soon slipping from earth's hold—

     The burnt sound of that departure.

◊

Grief of wasps, their long marches from the stomachs of the dead, their sleek coats and white scarves, for such grief I am sorry. Crumbling creek bank, sheared cliffs, deer that come from the woods in gray mist, tenderly crossing the spit of field singly and in bunches until I whistle the stray dog sending them, white tail flags flashing, leaping to trees. The whistle. The dog. Who seems to know nothing of death. I am sorry. For knowing too much of death. For all those nights I did not go out. For all the nights I did. But always for the wrong reasons to the wrong places with the wrong people. Or with no one. No one at all. I'm sorry. Oh cat killed by coyotes. Oh orange cat, marked with sorrow's flame, cat content with dirt, summon the other world, lift me, show me the way to the river.

◊

Blue camas or death camas,
wild lily or purple-stemmed hemlock,

young leaves of pokeberry
or the common nightshade. Swamp saxifrage

or dogbane. Waterleafs or baneberries.
I don't know what I can eat, what will kill me.

What of this hollow stem, this leaf, hairy and toothed?

◊

True, here loblolly and pitch pine stretch straight up,
and chinquapin and black tupelo fight for sun.
Here sycamore sheds its bark to a shined, gnarled
white trunk and the woods' floor, leaf meal and mulch,

is cast in branched shadow. Dragonflies, the fine tempered
metal of their split mouths hinging open, explode
into the insect-throbbing world. And flowers: beds
of echinacea, stokesia, coreopsis, and tritoma,

its many-mouthed and yellow-tongued single stalk

the ruby-throated hummingbirds sink their beaks into all day.
True, here, the blue-misted mountains stretch across the horizon.
Gray and black thunderheads swirled green,
sweep in and the earth's water rises to meet the rain
which sheets straight down like waterfalls but just like in magic

places of story books, the storms lift, clouds tear apart
like cotton candy and the sun unfurls
like tumbling bolts of silk so that great stretches of land tremble
in luminous air and steam rises off the backs of horses,

fence posts, tree limbs and elderberry
with their milky saucers of flowers.
True, great beauty is here. Cinnamon ferns, flats
of gaillardia and columbine, blazing stars uncurling

purple fronds as if they meant to anchor the earth
in its travels through the galaxy. True, all of that,
but also a woman, in hammered pain,

legs like joists that won't align in their sockets,
a puckered scar in the small of her back
and no money for food, a woman who hasn't eaten,
                  true, this too, in sixteen days.

◊

True also, what I have heard:
  on the seventeenth day
of no food
        you leave ground,
  float a foot
        above gravel and grass,
  a foot above
        the mere, mortal world.

◊

1933, Ex-President Hoover fishing:

A local man led him to a shack.
Nobody is actually starving, President Hoover had said,
the hoboes are better fed than they've ever been, but
in the shack lay one child
                                        dead,
seven others
                        nearly so.

And now the dead child twirls underground and for
the seven who are left, each bite of food is a sorrow,
each breeze through corn silks is her name
echoed up from its crowded room of roots.

She's the blight and the black spot, the freeze
and thaw buckling the hard clay, last and first

frost, seed-lipped weeds, spider mites, luminescent
powder smeared into the grit of your hands.

And the dead, safe in their fuzzy coffins,
lie back and rock in the day's heat.

◊

Fingers run along ribs,
                        light breaking against them like music
before it's swallowed in the hole where there used to be a heart,
that hollow place that tosses out moths
to beat against the back of her gritted teeth.

◊

It's not hunger from which one dies but despair
or so the night comes, with its smell of owls and blood,

to tell me. Seeds thrown to dry clay
and fields left to rising water and pondweed, it tells me.

On swollen feet from days at the loom in the rheumed light

of cotton mills, night says,
as the white-haired children lie down clutching their last breaths.

And my father,
                    here he comes,
a floppy-eared Bassett trotting behind him,

here to tell me not to give up, here to tell me
of his days of hunger, nine-year-old, hopping trains in 1929,

begging work, here to tell me, the body's an amazing thing,
now that he doesn't have one, he should know.

It can take years to die, he's here to say. He wants me
to know that was what most surprised him.

Though he doesn't know if he broke
ground or the ground broke him,

the trees like the question and pitch it
back and forth high in their feathered branches.

◊

Now in this second year in the greenhouse,
            I become cadmium, a cold-boned forest, bare limbs.
                        That scratch against sky.

Silent moment before the storm breaks, yellow wind.

Mist rising from the frozen pond, skirl of melting
ice, rain running along roots to quartz and clay.

Kicked from mud, I climb the arrowroot plant
and sing to the breaking clouds, sing
to the sky scudded blue. Dirt. Splatter of sun

through trees. The grit taste of it, box turtle thrusting
up from under leaf and mulch, through scrub
and litter. I tunnel blind under the surface thunder.

The queen bumble bee fumbles from the rock crevice,
pollen-smeared, pollen-gorged, and searches hollow roots
and mouse burrows for a nesting site.

I am that hole, that emptiness waiting. I am the hundreds of lives
  inside her.

Smell of the earth warming, water rising, soil stirring.
The subtle salt of the creek rushing toward its own end.

Cattail, Bugbane, Bloodroot, Trillium, Lady's Slippers
pulsing into light, the thrum of that deep in the earth.

Dragonfly nymphs pushed forward by water
shooting from their abdomens,
grasping the cattail stalk. That slow clumsy climb,
light filtering past, bodies still breathing water,
then the slow split up the back as they leap to sew
the air with color.

I am all of that.

And all the fluttered amoeba, multi-armed and slender
as pickerel weed, contracting and expanding in a sinuous lunge.
Algae slipping up rock faces, creatures so small
they live years
rising from the pond's bottom to the scummed surface.
Clustered thousands, their intricate shapes, hexagons and triangles,
many-hued and prismatic, the millions of lives that I have become,
the great secret encased in a single pinch of earth.

◊

Because the moths yammered all night, beating the blood-black air
with dusty wings, their eyes neon-red in moonlight. Because the
night-blooming angel's trumpets shiver when the moths bare their
sharpened teeth. Because twenty-two days is too long to go without
food. Because. Because.

94

Even the Io moths refuse to teach me the truth of hunger but leave their larvae to shred the corn, chewing it to stalk and stubble, spinning thin cocoons across the stricken fields.

Because no one speaks to me under the cucumbers' vining, no one joins me in praise of the pumpkins' bristled leaves, those green platters of promise, because the moths cling to my face, tap my teeth with their antennae, whisper their pollen-hunger to my wormy heart.

◊

Thinking now of the sheer numbers, the river-lonely,
the poor who walk into the night, slip between
buildings, shrink into themselves, use up
all their light and disappear into the countless
thick-tongued dead, the dead who even now
slosh themselves from sleep and gather
their feathers, names stuck somewhere deep in their throats.

But what would happen if just one person,
before tumbling into that beak-toothed night,
should spit out her name,
                          should become visible?

When will it come at last, this strange thing we call
death, this black river, no wind, birds screaming night terrors,
strange rustlings, rasp of metal on metal,
tin roof bending, owl lifting from its secret branch,
hunger waiting in its stone coat, licking its many lips.

From the all-night deli, the 24-hour Laundromat,
bus stations and steam grates, into rivers and out of rivers,
a dime, a nickel, three pennies lolling spider-eyed
in her left pants pocket, she having leapt into the flame
of homelessness' shame, down the river-lonely street.

And from the river she comes.

When her face rises outside your window,
oh, do not say, raccoons in the trash,

do not roll over in your sleep and mumble acorns
on the roof, squirrels in the attic.

When cakes fall in the oven, when a sudden swift
wind sweeps eddies of dust and leaf meal into your house,
when luna moths batter against your screen,
lightning bugs flit room to room, bats drop

down your chimney and birds ease through eaves,
oh, whatever deranged and wild beast has come
from the dark edge of the forest, whatever stories
it secrets deep inside its beak, know, oh, please, know, always,

                                                            it is she.

◊

Fluted vases, tumbled bells yawned open to air and rain,
tongues crawling with bees, lampshades flipped upright.

These yellow flowers, trumpeting their songs of cocozelle,
cucumber and crook-necked squash into the world.

Nothing has changed except this:
From this pinch of yellow, this flat-faced
delicate flower, a nub of green,

and two days later, the knobby cucumber,
now pinky-thick and nearly as long.

◊

Hours I sit on the oil-stained oak bench, my one pair
of dress slacks cinched at the new notch I knifed
in the belt this morning. All cases go against
the defendants. Phone bills, traffic tickets, rental disputes.
The Honorable Judge nearly out of his seat
yelling at whichever miserable cull cowers
before him, the young black man who hasn't paid
his phone bill, *over charged,* he says, *their mistake,* he says,

tries out the phrase, *your honor,* though you can see
by his face it's like sour spit in his mouth.

You're disrespecting my court, his honor shouts,
face shiny with sweat. *Don't come to my court
in shorts,* he repeats to the tanned, sun-bleached blond
in knee-length, khaki Dockers, clean and creased,
his Izod shirt tucked, black belt, spit-shiny.
He'd come straight from work, couldn't afford
to miss the day of work, he says again and again.
The case goes against him

though he has two witnesses, three against the word
of one policeman. Just this morning I limped
to the outdoor water pump, raised and dropped
its squeaky lever once, twice, and sprayed
myself, squeezing the tight nozzle, adjusting
the spray mist, washing my hair, shoulders, breasts,
running my hands along the concave curve of my belly,
thighs, calves, feet with water which had waited cool

and coiled in the hose all night, unscrewing the coupling,
cupping my hands to drink the old copper stink, the spurts
of water hours later I can still feel sloshing
in my gut, this twenty-fifth day without food, as I slump,
dizzy, on the hard bench, rechecking the safety pin,
the popped-off button hidden under the knife-notched belt.

◊

In nearly a year, mid-winter, I will
read the newspaper headline, *Hospital
Makes Record Twenty Million Profit.* In nearly a year,
the greenhouse hunkered down in two feet
of snow, I will pull on socks worn to a thin
shine, then slip into trash bags pulled and tied
past my calves, and over the slick of that cold
plastic, I will pull on wet Keds and, footprints
staggering behind me like small graves,
I will leave the greenhouse, walk west

past the mounds of stubbled coneflowers
and gallairdia, past the bare-branched twigs
of peonies, through the barbed wire glittering
in ice, across the pasture and toward what seems
another world, one in which there is no sound,
deer hummocked under the snow-felled boughs of pine,
bobcat and coyote dug into the soft ground, leaving
only a rocky creek, a quiet muscle that will circle this valley,
then ease east to become a river, then silently move
through the season, banks edged in snow, to the ocean
and its own death. And from the river I come.

Autumn in the Heart

All day ashes sift down like dry snow
to settle in fields and coat the creek and pond
and grind into the porous opening of all things.

Even my own blood slows
under this darkened, ash-hammered sky.

◊

In Chinese calligraphy, autumn in the heart is sorrow,
                                        sun going down,
flowers heavy with seed, cucumbers swollen
and yellow on the vine, trees felled and burned,
the paper company's two-thousand acres sold—
                                        a gated community,
half-a-million dollar house every half acre, eighteen-hole golf course.
Already the bulldozers crash through the woods
paving out horse trails and nature walks.

◊

The sky eases down and all the particularities
of land vanish in corpse-light. No revelation,
no answer in the spiders spinning in their webbed cages,
no answer in the frog grunting under the bed
or in this birch, lightning struck, shattered,
split root to crown, two years in a row
sending out shoots all along its trunk.

But what can this birch say now in the endless
revving of chainsaws, what can it say
to these years spent in a greenhouse,
years gone now, tumbled into the star-wheeling sky?

Ashes light on the horses restless in the fields, drift
over the salvia and astilbe, sift across the aster and scabiosa,

and catch on the leaves so that the trees are forced to bear this last
indignity, burnt remnants of felled trees filling the sky,
                                        ashes floating like lost children to their arms.

Elegy

As the creek clogs with mud, as trillium,
calypso, and lady's slippers lift into the dozer's
gaped mouth, as pileated woodpeckers
sink beaks into the widow makers' rotted hearts,
as the kingfisher hovers above the silt-thick water
for the last time, then beats across the sedge
and saw-grass heavy with seed toward the blue scar
in the east as sun enters a mist-beaded web, the spider,
gone now, having swung from the maple's top branch
to stitch a stretch of wind to the pokeberry,
top heavy, laden with dark fruit, first light
slant in the distance, rain just ended, fog curling
from the fields' ruts and shallows, a rabbit freezing
in a hawk's shadow as the chainsaw revs
to a high-pitched scream, I feel it,
the earth shaking loose, groaning to a halt,
feel it shudder and roll off its one great root.

Tomorrow the Day Comes Alone

After the chainsaw, after the pond fills with silt
and mud, after the land washes from itself
with each rain, after the slow suffocation
of the copepods, no-legged and eight-legged,
antennae, long as their bodies, trailing behind
them, no longer will the clear rotifers, gut gears
like watch works, rise from the pond's ooze and muck.

Whirligig beetles, one eye watching below, one
above, will no longer scuff or scratch the water's surface.

Dragon and damselfly nymphs: no longer
will they shake from their bodies like ghosts.

Already the rainbows and creek chubs, red bellies
and bullheads sink to the pond's bottom
faster than the topsoil pushed before each storm.

Already the leopard frogs and spadefoot toads,
pickerels and spring peepers, cricket frogs, dusky salamanders
and red-spotted newts bury themselves for the last time.

Harvest mice no longer nibble the milkweed's silk-parachuted
seeds and golden mice do not clamber to their round nests
in the loblolly pine's moon-tipped branches.

Bobcats have left their hollow trees, foxes their burrowed banks,
ache of starvation twisting muscles and polishing bone.

No more robber-faced raccoon padding from the woods'
edge, no more opossum, paws like gloves of padded leather.

No more deer leaping the wire in the far field
to glide toward the garden. None of us turn
in our restless nights to the whisks of their breath
and know they are with us.

Trees crumble to the ground. Woodpeckers cry out
and we are alone, only our hunger and the sun
glaring down on this stripped and burnt land.

Scream of metal on wood, smoke of green trees.
Because we came as if we believed this land vacant,

never again will we know in each kicked up leaf,
or in each footprint, the thousands of lives held there.

ABOUT JUDY JORDAN

Judy Jordan's first book of poetry, *Carolina Ghost Woods*, won the 1999 Walt Whitman Award from the Academy of American Poets, the 2000 National Book Critics Circle Award, as well as the Utah Book of the Year Award, the OAY Award from the Poetry Council of North Carolina, and the Thomas Wolfe Literary Award. Her second book of poetry, *Sixty Cent Coffee and a Quarter to Dance*, was published by LSU press. Jordan just completed a fourth book of poetry, *Children of Salt*, and is currently working on a fifth and sixth manuscript. Jordan built her own environmentally friendly house out of cob and earthbag while living in a tent, founded SIPRAW, which rescued dogs out of puppy mills, lives off the grid, and teaches creative writing at Southern Illinois University, Carbondale.

Her work has appeared in numerous journals (including *Alaska Quarterly Review, Crossroads: A Journal of Southern Culture, Ellipsis, Gulf Coast, Plume, Poetry, Prime Mincer,* and *Western Humanities Review*) and anthologies (including *American Poetry: The Next Generation, Faith & Doubt: An Anthology of Poems, Southern Poetry Anthology Volume III: Contemporary Appalachia*, and Upper Rubber Boot's *Apocalypse Now: Poems and Prose from the End of Days*).

ACKNOWLEDGEMENTS

Judy Jordan would like to thank the following journals, where poems in *Hunger* first appeared: *Atticus Review* ("Elegy," *Pushcart* nominee), Connotation Press' *An Online Artifact* ("These First Mornings Living in the Greenhouse,","Night Walk, After Surgery, October"), *kysoflash* ("Autumn in the Heart"), *Longish Poems* ("Into Light, Into Another Day," "After the Farmer's Market"), and *New South Journal* ("Hunger Moon," *Pushcart* nominee).

ABOUT THE EDITOR

Andrew McFadyen-Ketchum is a poet, professional editor, and educator living in Denver, CO. He is the author of a collection of poems, *Ghost Gear*; series editor of *Floodgate Poetry Series: Three Chapbooks by Three Poets in a Single Volume*; editor of *Apocalypse Now: Poems and Prose from the End of Days*; editor of *Warning! Poems May Be Longer That They Appear: An Anthology of Long-ish Poems* (forthcoming); and founder and managing editor of PoemoftheWeek.org. Read his work and learn more at AndrewMK.com.

OTHER BOOKS BY UPPER RUBBER BOOT

Anthologies:

140 And Counting: an anthology of writing from 7x20, Joanne Merriam, ed.
Apocalypse Now: Poems and Prose from the End of Days, Andrew McFadyen-Ketchum and Alexander Lumans, eds.
Choose Wisely: 35 Women Up To No Good, H. L. Nelson and Joanne Merriam, eds.
How to Live on Other Planets: A Handbook for Aspiring Aliens, Joanne Merriam, ed.

Fiction:

Bicycle Girl: a short story, Tade Thompson
Changing the World: a short story, David M. Harris
Heist: a short story, Tracy Canfield
Flight 505: a novella, Leslie Bohem
Johnny B: a short story, Phil Voyd
The Mask Game, Sergey Gerasimov
Memory: a novelette, Teresa P. Mira de Echeverría (Lawrence Schimel, trans.)
The Selves We Leave Behind: a short story, Shira Lipkin
Signs Over the Pacific and Other Stories, RJ Astruc
The Suicide Inspector: a short story, J. J. Steinfeld
The Tortoise Parliament: a short story, Kenneth Schneyer
Twittering the Stars: a short story, Mari Ness
The Widow and the Xir: a short story, Indrapramit Das

Poetry:

Blueshifting, Heather Kamins
Floodgate Poetry Series, edited by Andrew McFadyen-Ketchum
The Glaze from Breaking, Joanne Merriam
Hiss of Leaves, T. D. Ingram
Marilyn Monroe: Poems, Lyn Lifshin
Measured Extravagance, Peg Duthie
The Sky Needs More Work, Corey Mesler

COPYRIGHT INFORMATION

Floodgate Poetry Series Vol. 2
ISBN 978-1-937794-38-5
©2015 of respective authors

Cover art by NASA/Bill Ingalls
Cover design by Joanne Merriam

Published in the United States of America